CHOLERA

Curse of the Nineteenth Century

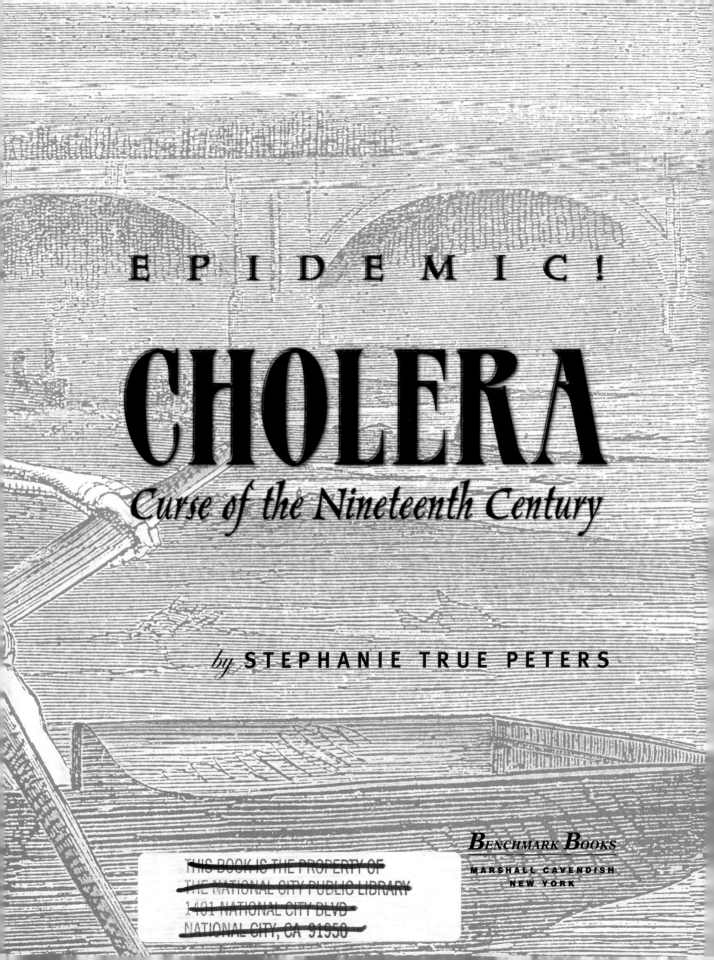

E P I D E M I C !

CHOLERA

Curse of the Nineteenth Century

by STEPHANIE TRUE PETERS

BENCHMARK BOOKS

MARSHALL CAVENDISH
NEW YORK

ACKNOWLEDGMENTS

With thanks to Allison Kavey, Lecturer, Department of the History of Science, Medicine, and Technology, Johns Hopkins University, Baltimore, for her careful reading of the manuscript.

Benchmark Books
Marshall Cavendish
99 White Plains Road
Tarrytown, New York 10591-9001
www.marshallcavendish.com

Copyright © 2005 by Marshall Cavendish Corporation

All Internet sites were available and accurate when this book was sent to press.

Book design by Michael Nelson

LIBRARY OF CONGRESS CATALOGING-IN-PUBLICATION DATA

Peters, Stephanie True, 1965-
Cholera / by Stephanie True Peters.
p. cm. — (Epidemic!)
Includes bibliographical references and index.
ISBN 0-7614-1634-X
1. Cholera—History—Juvenile literature. I. Title
II. Series: Peters, Stephanie True, 1965- . Epidemic!.
RC127.P48 2004
614.5'14—dc22
2004000844

Picture Research by Linda Sykes Picture Research, Inc., Hilton Head, S. C.

Photo credits: Back cover, x, 2, 12, 14, 15, 16, 17, 18, 20, 32, 33, 38, 46, 48, Mary Evans Picture Library; front cover: Musee du Chateau de Versailles/Dagli Orti/The Art Archive; ii, ii, 6, 8, 10, 25, 36, 41, 50, 53, The Granger Collection; vii: Domenica del Corriere/Dagli Orti/The Art Archive; viii: Hulton Archive/Getty Images; 4, 5: Hermitage, St. Petersburg, Russia/ Bridgeman Art Library; 23: Sunderland Art Galleries, Tye and Wear, UK/ Bridgeman Art Library; 24: AKG, London; 28: Victoria and Albert Museum, London, UK/Bridgeman Art Library; 29: Guildhall Library, Corp. of London, UK/Bridgeman Art Library; 34: Musee d'Histoire de la Medecine, Paris, France/Charmet/Bridgeman Art Library; 42 Hulton Archive/Getty Images; 55 (top), 55 (bottom): The Stapleton Collection/Bridgeman Art Library; 57: Gustavo Gilabert/Corbis SABA; 60: Chris Hondros/Getty Images

PRINTED IN CHINA

1 3 5 6 4 2

Front cover: 19th-century French painting of a doctor, nurse, and patient
Back cover: Early 20th-century painting of an industrial town: Sheffield, England
Half title: "Death's Dispensary": 19th-century English cartoon linking cholera to drinking water
Title page: 19th-century English cartoon of Death navigating the polluted Thames
From the Author, page vii: Cholera victims in Istanbul, Turkey

CONTENTS

FROM THE AUTHOR

The idea for a series of books about epidemics came to me while I was sitting in the doctor's office with my son. He had had a sleepless, feverish night. I suspected he had an ear infection and looked forward to the doctor confirming my diagnosis and prescribing antibiotics.

While waiting for the doctor to appear, I suddenly realized that the situation I was in—a mother looking to relieve her child's pain—was hardly new. Humans have had an ongoing battle against disease throughout history. Today, we have tremendous knowledge of how the human body works. We understand how viruses and bacteria attack and how the body defends itself. Through immunizations and simple hygiene, we're often able to prevent disease in the first place. Our ancestors were not so knowledgeable, nor so lucky.

In this series, I have tried to put a human face on five epidemics that laid millions low. All five occurred in the past and have since been medically controlled. Yet in some areas of the world, similar stories are still being played out today as humans struggle against such enemies as AIDS, Ebola virus, hantavirus, and other highly contagious diseases. In the fight against disease, we may never have the upper hand. Microscopic foes are hard to fight.

A sailor fumigates a ship after its arrival in the French port of Marseille during the cholera outbreak of 1884. Before the cause of the disease was understood, people thought it was possible to prevent cholera by sterilizing an area with smoke.

THE UNINVITED DINNER GUEST

In March of 1991, a New Jersey man flew home from Ecuador. Among his belongings was a package of crabmeat he had purchased while in South America. A few days later, the man invited several friends and family members to dinner. The meal included a salad made with the crabmeat. Within days of the meal, everyone who had attended the dinner party came down with severe diarrhea. Five people also began vomiting. Three experienced excruciating leg cramps. Five became so ill they were hospitalized.

Doctors quickly treated the patients for dehydration and gave them antibiotics to fight infection. They also began searching for the cause of the illness. They soon had their answer. In some of the patients' stool samples, they found *Vibrio cholerae,* the bacterium that causes the disease cholera. The source of the bacteria was the crabmeat. Everyone from the dinner party eventually made a full recovery, thanks to the prompt treatment they received. Not everyone who contracts cholera is so lucky.

Millions of people worldwide have died of the disease. The worst epidemics occurred in the nineteenth century, before the cause of cholera was identified and treatments developed. Those epidemics, and the conditions that allowed them to occur, are the subjects of this book. The story of cholera does not end at the close of the nineteenth century, however. Although the disease is no longer a mystery, it continues to kill thousands each year.

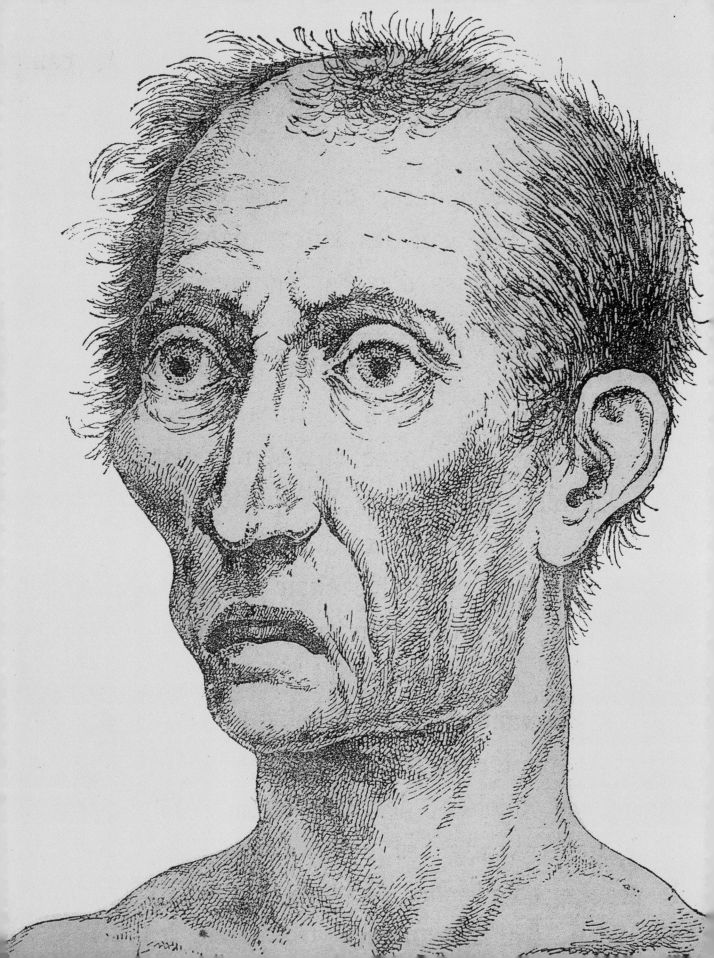

CHAPTER ONE

WHAT IS CHOLERA?

❧

I ONCE MARKED DOWN AS DEAD AN INDIVIDUAL
WHO IN FACT DIED ONLY SEVERAL HOURS LATER.
—*French doctor, 1832, commenting on*
the deathlike appearance
of cholera victims

HE STORY OF CHOLERA BEGINS IN THE WATERS of the Ganges River in India. The Ganges is vital to the people who live on the Indian subcontinent. It is a primary source of water, the focal point of social gatherings, and the inspiration for many of the beliefs of the Hindu religion. For centuries Indians have flocked to its banks to bathe, get drinking and cooking water, wash their food and clothes, and participate in religious ceremonies and festivals.

The Ganges is also home to the bacterium known as *Vibrio cholerae*, the microscopic organism that causes cholera. A small outbreak of cholera, unless quickly brought under control, can turn into an epidemic or, even, a pandemic.

Opposite:
Cholera victims
waste away until
their faces are
death masks.

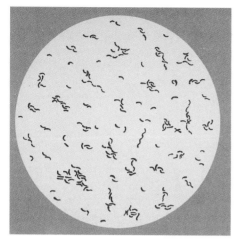

Comma-shaped
Vibrio cholerae,
as seen under
a microscope

Epidemics spread rapidly, affecting a large number of people in one area or community. If an epidemic is allowed to continue unchecked, it can become a pandemic—a widespread outbreak of a disease that affects several parts of the world at the same time.

Prior to 1817, it is believed, cholera epidemics occurred only in the region around the Ganges River. Then, in that year, the disease broke out of its traditional borders, beginning the first of seven pandemics. To understand how and why cholera was able to spread beyond the Ganges, one must first understand the nature of *V. cholerae*.

V. CHOLERAE

V. cholerae is a water-borne bacterium shaped like a comma. It has one or two tails that thrash and help it move. It is harmless to humans until it has been ingested. Once in the digestive system, however, it can cause severe illness—even death—within hours. When the bacteria reach the small intestine, they begin to multiply rapidly. As they do, they release a powerful toxin that causes the cells of the intestinal wall to secrete more fluids than normal. The first symptoms of cholera are diarrhea and vomiting. Victims of severe cholera infection excrete an enormous volume of watery stool in very little time—sometimes as much as one quart of fluid an hour. This stool is commonly described as "rice water" because of the white particles that fleck the fluid. These particles are actually tiny bits of intestinal lining. Along with these bits, water, salts, and other substances literally flow out of the body. If the diarrhea and vomiting continue untreated, the victim becomes seriously dehydrated and spirals into a rapid decline.

Dehydration causes the skin, mouth, and eyes to dry out. The circulatory system struggles to pump blood throughout the body. Body temperature and blood pressure drop quickly. The victim's pulse becomes rapid, weak, and thready. Soon the skin takes on a bluish hue. As fluids continue to gush out of the body, the flesh around the eyes sinks in and the lips pull back from the teeth, turning the face into a death mask. Muscles cramp, sometimes leading to paralysis or violent and uncontrolled spasms.

These symptoms can be reversed if the patient is quickly given the right kind of fluids to replace those that have been lost. Since it can be difficult for someone vomiting to keep anything down, most modern cholera treatments pump fluids back into the body through a small tube inserted into a vein under the skin.

Without this fluid replacement, the victim's kidneys will shut down. The job of the kidneys is to filter out impurities from the bloodstream and send them to the bladder in the form of urine. Kidneys that have shut down no longer clean the blood, so poisonous waste products build up in the victim's weakened circulatory system. At this point in the disease, the patient typically goes into shock and slips into a coma, or dies.

Interestingly, not all people who ingest *V. cholerae* become ill. Some show no symptoms at all; others display only mild symptoms. Sometimes, the patient hasn't swallowed enough of the bacteria to do harm. Other times, the acid content of the infected person's stomach lessens the severity of the disease by killing the bacteria before they arrive in the small intestine. And some lucky people seem to have a natural

In this nineteenth-century illustration, people flee the deathlike figure of Cholera, who arrives in town packing a sharp scythe to mow down his victims.

resistance to the disease. However, even though these people do not suffer from cholera, they still carry the bacteria within their bodies.

Direct person-to-person transmission of the disease is rare, but an infected person can spread cholera indirectly. Cholera bacteria travel by oral-fecal routes; that is, they enter the body by the mouth and leave the body in feces. When an infected person excretes waste into a communal water supply or handles food without washing his hands thoroughly after going to the bathroom, he introduces the bacteria into the water or onto the food, contaminating it. When others ingest this water or food, they run the risk of becoming infected and continuing the contamination cycle.

Cholera bacteria thrive in water polluted by human waste and sewage. They have also been found in certain kinds of foods, such as rice and shellfish that come from waters containing the bacteria. To avoid contracting cholera, one should steer clear of food and water that may be contaminated. Also, foods should always be properly washed.

THE HISTORY OF CHOLERA

Historians believe that cholera has long been endemic, or always present in low levels, in the region surrounding the Ganges. Ancient Indian texts dating from 400 B.C. describe a disease many scholars think was cholera. An inscription on an Indian monolith dating from the same time period reads, "the lips blue, the face haggard, the eyes hollow, the stomach sunk in, the limbs contracted and crumpled as if by fire, those are the signs of the great illness." These symptoms sound very much like cholera.

During the centuries that cholera roamed the Ganges River area, Europeans were largely unaware of the disease. Doctors hadn't heard about it since they did not have much contact with India. Then, in the mid-eighteenth century, England began to colonize

Cholera spread to Europe after Europeans colonized India.

the subcontinent. Colonization brought soldiers, settlers, and merchants. By the early nineteenth century, as contact with India increased, doctors in Europe began to see their first cases of the dreaded disease.

Cholera moved beyond the borders of India in 1817. The first recorded pandemic of the disease seems to have had its roots in a three-month-long Hindu festival that took place along the Upper Ganges. During this festival, people from all over India gathered at the river. They bathed in its waters, drank from it, and eliminated their wastes in it.

After the festival ended, they returned to their homes in various parts of the country. Many showed the classic signs of cholera infection, including uncontrollable diarrhea and vomiting. Others carried cholera bacteria with them in their guts without knowing it. Their wastes contaminated the drinking waters of their regions. Soon cholera cropped up in many different places in India. Calcutta, a major city and home to many foreign merchants, colonists, and soldiers, as well as

Indians, was caught up in a full-scale epidemic. Deaths numbered in the hundreds of thousands.

From Calcutta and other parts of India, *V. cholerae* made its way along trade routes to other countries. It journeyed in the intestines of soldiers and seamen, merchants and ordinary travelers—and in barrels of contaminated drinking water. Southeast Asia, China, Egypt, Persia, eastern Russia—all became infected in a pandemic that lasted until 1824. The exact death toll is not known, but estimates place it in the millions. The number might have been even higher had not a particularly severe Russian winter stopped the disease in its tracks.

A second pandemic began a mere two years after the first ended. Again, it started in India and followed the same paths as the 1817 outbreak. But this time cold weather did not kill

CHOLERA *Curse of the Nineteenth Century*

the bacteria. Instead, cholera made its first appearance in Europe, arriving in 1830 and terrifying people with its deadly ferocity. From Europe it continued on to North America, striking the major cities of that continent from 1832 to 1834 before dying out.

Five years later the third pandemic began its march around the world. British troops residing in India carried *V. cholerae* to Afghanistan in 1839. A year later China was hit. When the pandemic finally died down in 1848, it had reached across Asia, Europe, and North and South America. Once again, deaths numbered in the hundreds of thousands.

Cholera began its fourth worldwide journey in 1854, its fifth in 1863, its sixth in 1881, and its seventh in 1961. The pandemics brought fear and misery wherever they occurred. During the last three outbreaks, however, people's fears were soothed somewhat by the fact that doctors in Europe had discovered the cause of the disease and understood how it was transmitted. Thanks to this knowledge, the physicians had the means to control cholera's spread and to help its victims.

In 1854, however, they had no such knowledge. Doctors were at a loss to explain how the dread disease, virtually unknown to them less than forty years earlier, had found such a solid foothold in their countries.

CHAPTER TWO

LIFE IN THE TIME OF CHOLERA

☙❧

WHERE GARBAGE AND FILTH OF EVERY DESCRIPTION
ARE LEFT ON THE SURFACE TO FERMENT AND ROT;
WHERE POOLS OF STAGNANT WATER ARE ALMOST CONSTANT;
WHERE DWELLINGS ADJOINING ARE THUS NECESSARILY CAUSED
TO BE OF AN INFERIOR AND EVEN FILTHY DESCRIPTION;
THUS WHERE DISEASE IS ENGENDERED,
AND THE HEALTH OF THE WHOLE TOWN PERILLED.

—from a report on the conditions of the town of
Hudderfield, England, early 1800s

ONG BEFORE CHOLERA MADE ITS WAY out of India to Europe, some Europeans had made their way into India. For hundreds of years, merchants had been buying and selling goods from the great Asian subcontinent. By the 1400s, European countries were competing with one another for control of the riches that lay within India's borders. Spices, tea, fine fabrics, and other commodities abounded in the East—and Europeans were hungry for them all.

By the middle of the eighteenth century, Great Britain had won control of India, squeezing out competition from France and the Netherlands. India was not the only region to become subject to Great Britain. South Africa, Australia, and parts of

Opposite:
Crowded slums—
a result of the
Industrial
Revolution—were
fertile breeding
grounds for disease.

China were all British possessions in the eighteenth century. So too were the American colonies until they gained their independence in 1783.

As raw materials and goods poured in from these territories, Great Britain became one of the wealthiest countries in the world. This wealth allowed England to spearhead the greatest and swiftest economic change of all times—the Industrial Revolution.

THE INDUSTRIAL REVOLUTION

By the mid-1700s England was in prime position to change from a mainly agricultural society to an industrial one. Many people had profited from the nation's colonial possessions, and these wealthy merchants and gentry were willing to invest money in new business ventures. The money they invested helped foster the nation's entrepreneurial spirit. Innovative minds developed inventions that led to the growth of many industries. Chief among these were the textile, iron, and coal industries.

The textile industry was the first to undergo a major change. Before the 1750s, merchants bought raw materials and took them to workers living in cottages on farms or in villages. Some workers spun the materials, such as wool or cotton, into yarn while others wove the yarn into cloth. These small home-based "cottage industries," as they came to be called, dotted the countryside. Then, inventions such as the spinning jenny came along and revolutionized the cloth industry. The new machines dramatically improved the quality and quantity of yarn and changed how cloth was made. When these machines became too large and numerous to fit into ordinary homes, they were housed in large buildings—the first mills and factories. As demand for high-quality cloth rose, so did the need for workers to run the machines. Towns with textile factories grew rapidly as people moved from the country to take these new jobs.

Not long after the cloth industry took off, the British iron and coal industries also experienced a growth spurt. Coal and iron were intricately intertwined. Coal was used to heat iron to make it easier to work with. Iron was used to manufacture tools that made it easier to get coal out of the ground. Improvements to one industry invariably led to the growth of the other.

As iron became easier to use, inventors, engineers, and mechanics turned to this metal to create and improve their machines. "It is by iron fingers, teeth, and wheels . . . that the cotton is opened, cleaned, spread, carded, drawn, roved, spun, wound, warped, dressed, and woven," one person observed. The demand for iron products and machine parts created new jobs for laborers, miners, and skilled ironworkers. The mining workforce swelled, and towns near the iron and coal industries tripled in size.

As its industries grew, England made improvements to the nation's road and canal networks. Better roads and canals made it easier to transport the raw materials and workers to the factories, and to get the manufactured goods to the people who wanted to buy them.

Cities like Manchester, England, tripled in size during the Industrial Revolution.

Laborers of both sexes filled factories by the late 1800s.

The growth of all industries was accelerated by the development of the steam engine. Crude steam engines had powered pumps to drain water out of coal mines as early as 1712. In 1769, the engine's design was improved. By the early 1800s steam power was replacing waterpower as the driving force behind most machinery.

Steam engines made a huge impact on trade and transportation as well. At first, the engines were used to move small cargo boats through England's waterways. Later, they powered the huge locomotives of trains, thus giving birth to England's railway industry.

Transportation by train took the country by storm. As of 1838, Britain had laid five hundred miles of track. By 1848, that number had grown to five thousand miles. Thousands of laborers, including a large workforce of immigrants from Ireland, found jobs making railway parts, carving the land to make way for the rails, and laying track. This workforce was very mobile, moving around the country to wherever its labor was needed and increasing the population of certain areas for a time before it moved on to the next location.

In a span of only about one hundred years, Great Britain had become the most industrialized society in the world. But many other countries, including Belgium, France, Germany, and the United States, were not far behind. Most borrowed ideas, machines, and skilled workers from England to build their own versions of textile, coal, iron, and railway industries. Like England, they saw the value of improving their road and canal systems and upgrading their fleets of cargo ships. By the late 1800s much of Europe and the United States had joined England as fully industrialized societies. Cities grew up almost overnight, modeled on England's industrial towns in almost every way—good and bad.

SLUM LIFE

Few cities of the nineteenth century were designed to handle the number of people who packed into them. Sewage and sanitation systems, drinking water supplies, and housing in particular were inadequate. In general, cities were filthy, polluted, and overcrowded.

Many cities had very limited systems for collecting trash. In fact, herds of swine were often the only means of ridding streets of the garbage that accumulated outside most dwellings. This garbage mingled with human waste dumped from chamber pots. The vile mixture turned into putrid, bacteria-infested sludge that clogged street gutters. The sludge was so thick in some areas that not even a heavy rain could wash it away.

To make matters worse, outdated sewer systems were incapable of handling the sudden increase in human waste made by the ever-growing population. Filth from outhouses, or privies as they were called, leaked into the streets. In some areas, raw sewage emptied directly into nearby rivers, ditches, and wells—the source of most people's drinking water.

Air pollution from coal furnaces blanketed industrialized cities.

"It was more like watery mud than muddy water," wrote author and editor Henry Mayhew (1812–1887) of a ditch he observed in London. "As we gazed in horror at it, we saw drains and sewers emptying their filthy contents into it; we saw a whole tier of doorless privies in the open road, common to men and women, built over it; we heard bucket after bucket of filth splash into it. . . . We asked if they really did drink the water? The answer was, 'they were obliged to drink the ditch, without which they could beg a pailful or thieve a pailful of water.'"

Factories added their own form of pollution. The coal fires that ran the steam engines belched soot and smoke into the air. Leftover textile dyes, ash from fires, and other factory by-products contaminated rivers and communal water supplies.

Despite the horrendous living conditions of the cities, people continued to move to them in search of jobs. All these people needed places to live. A few factory owners designed entire villages for their workers to live, shop, pray, and be educated in, believing that well-cared-for laborers would be more productive.

Most workers, however, lived in hastily constructed tenements erected in the less desirable areas of towns. These buildings crowded one another for space and light. Often they were built around a courtyard that contained a single well and pump, the only source of water for the hundreds of people who lived in the neighborhood. These neighborhoods became the first city slums.

CHOLERA *Curse of the Nineteenth Century*

Slums were places of squalor. Corrupt land-lords jammed whole families into rooms barely large enough for two people. The worst rooms were in the cellars, where moisture and muck dripped from the streets down the walls after every rain. People slept on straw-filled mattresses or directly on floors strewn with hay. They shared their sleeping space with strangers as well as mice, rats, fleas, and other vermin. Diseases such as smallpox, tuberculosis, and typhus ran rampant. Food was often scarce, leaving many malnourished and vulnerable to sickness.

Conditions within many factories contributed to the ill health of the workers. Dust, lint, smoke, and soot clogged lungs and eyes. The din of heavy machinery left many hard of hearing. Harsh chemicals used in dyes and paints caused irreparable damage to the skin. Men, women, and children were on their feet for fourteen hours a day, laboring on machines that could mangle or kill in the blink of an eye.

Adults and children alike lived in squalor in the slums. People were sometimes forced to sleep in the streets.

POLITICS AND PUBLIC HEALTH

Despite such hazards, many people were glad to have their jobs. Industries were becoming increasingly mechanized. As machines replaced people, fewer workers were needed. Meanwhile, the populations of industry towns continued to grow. Competition for factory jobs became stiff and allowed many factory owners to pay workers lower wages—a job with low pay was better than no job at all. Finally, in addition to mechanization and growing populations, many countries and cities experienced periodic depressions caused by the insta-bility of the changing economy. During these depressions, factories would close down or lay off a large number of workers for weeks at a time.

As a result, the poor became poorer, and those who had once held steady jobs found themselves out on the street with little more than the ragged clothes on their backs. People stole or even killed to survive.

Early sanitation often went no further than catching rats.

The ruling classes and governments of most industrialized countries were slow to respond to the plight of the poor. Some governments simply refused to acknowledge that there was a problem. Others were too caught up in the drive for industrialization to consider how the working class was being affected. For some governments, ongoing political turmoil and war overshadowed issues of social reform. And finally, many in the upper classes ignored the poor because they believed the poor had brought their unwholesome conditions upon themselves through laziness and sinful behavior.

Many governments were equally slow to recognize the hazards to public health posed by filthy slum conditions and inadequate sewerage and sanitation systems. In the early 1800s, few governments saw the necessity of upgrading sewers or controlling waste removal. Funds that might have been spent on such projects were spent on other things.

In addition, few governments had established national boards of health by this time. Without these boards, there were no centralized systems for monitoring public health or for responding to a health crisis. Those boards of health that did exist were undersized, disorganized, and limited in their power. The usual response to a public health crisis was to authorize local officials to use their own judgment and resources to handle it.

This policy worked up to a point, but it also meant that responses to problems differed from city to city depending on what local authorities believed was best for their own situation. The primary, and in many places only, response to a health crisis was quarantine.

Quarantine was the practice of isolating anyone or anything suspected of having or carrying a contagious disease. Individuals were confined to their homes, sometimes forcibly, to prevent them from spreading their illness to others. Incoming ships were isolated until all aboard were determined to be free of disease. Only when a ship was proven to be healthy was it allowed to dock and unload its cargo. Such quarantine measures had first been implemented some four hundred years before the Industrial Revolution began, in the wake of a horrifying epidemic of plague known to later generations as the Black Death (1347–1351). Quarantine remained the only means of preventing or controlling an epidemic up through the nineteenth century.

Before being allowed entry into a port, ships' passengers were quarantined for a period of time, to be sure they were free of disease.

Quarantine worked only when it was strictly enforced. Ordinary people, when put under quarantine by town officials, usually had no choice but to obey orders to stay confined in their homes. But when quarantine threatened to disrupt trade, businessmen could usually persuade corrupt health officials to look the other way long enough for ships to enter port and unload their cargo. Merchants also pressured or bribed officials to ignore, cover up, or misrepresent a health crisis if such a crisis meant a loss of profit.

Public health might have been taken more seriously had those most knowledgeable about health problems—the medical community—been a stronger, more unified force. But in the early 1800s, medicine was in a state of flux.

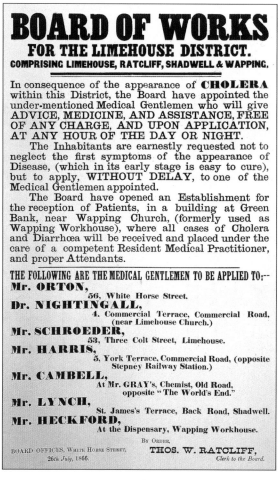

Public appeals urging cholera victims to see doctors were widespread by the mid-1800s.

THE MEDICAL COMMUNITY

In the early nineteenth century, physicians were struggling to gain public recognition, respect, and trust. Unfortunately at that time, standards for educating, training, and licensing doctors were minimal and followed no uniform system of instruction. In fact, just about anyone who had a mind to could set up a medical practice. A sick or injured person was just as likely to get treatment from an uneducated quack as from a trained professional. This situation did little to elevate the status of the medical community.

To complicate matters further, medical practitioners didn't always agree on how to approach medicine. Most clung to traditional notions of disease. Many believed that God sent sickness as punishment for sin or to test the strength of one's faith.

The most educated doctors had been taught that the body contained four humors: phlegm, blood, yellow bile, and black bile. Each humor had a certain property. Phlegm was cold and

CHOLERA *Curse of the Nineteenth Century*

wet, blood was hot and wet, yellow bile was hot and dry, and black bile was cold and dry. When the body's four humors were out of balance, the person became sick. Health was restored when the humors were brought back into balance. Bleeding a patient—opening a vein to release excess blood—was used to correct many humoral imbalances.

Alongside these theories was the belief that disease was transmitted by miasmas. Miasmas were poisonous clouds of foul-smelling air. Such clouds were born of cesspools, garbage heaps, decaying bodies, and other malodorous things. When a person became sick, it was because he or she had come into contact with the poisons within the cloud.

Finally, there was the theory of contagion. This theory stated that disease was spread through direct contact with the sick. When a healthy person touched a sick person, he or she picked up the disease-causing contagion and risked becoming ill with the same disease. As there was ample evidence for person-to-person transfer of many illnesses, this theory was gaining momentum in the nineteenth century.

The study of human anatomy and the practice of dissection, once stifled by the Church because they were considered defilements of the body, were commonplace by the early nineteenth century. Surgical practices also grew as knowledge of anatomy was put to use. As doctors became bolder, they experimented with new surgical techniques.

With so many differing opinions of how disease started and was spread, and the development of new ways of looking at the human body, it was nearly impossible for the medical community to agree on anything. This fact did little to raise the public's trust in doctors.

Reactions to the medical profession were mixed for other

Grave robbers stole bodies for anatomists to study.

reasons, too. While the wealthy might put their trust in the family doctor, the lower classes viewed the scientific community with suspicion. Such distrust was not unfounded. The corpses of the poor, not those of the rich, were usually the subjects of experiments. Students of anatomy got fresh cadavers from prisons and workhouses—and sometimes from body snatchers who desecrated the cemeteries of lower-class neighborhoods.

Hospitals and surgery were viewed with apprehension. Anesthesia was only introduced in the 1840s; antiseptics came into use in the 1860s. Until this time, most surgeons operated under unsanitary conditions, using dirty surgical instruments after rendering their patients unconscious with alcohol or blows to the head. Hospitals were filthy places where a patient was as likely to catch a deadly disease as to be cured of one. Many people were wary of entering hospitals or seeking any doctor's care, even in times of grave illness.

Deadly diseases such as tuberculosis, yellow fever, small-pox, and typhus had been around for generations and were still constantly testing medical knowledge. But doctors and patients alike knew what to expect from these feared but familiar illnesses. Therefore, when these diseases struck, the panic they caused was limited.

Not so when cholera appeared on the scene.

CHOLERA *Curse of the Nineteenth Century*

CHOLERA ARRIVES

When cholera came to Europe and the United States, it found conditions uniquely suited to its survival. It thrived in the polluted water sources and overtaxed sewer systems of the newly industrialized cities. It made itself at home in the crowded, filthy dwellings filled to bursting with downtrodden people. It raced around the countries along improved roads, newly laid railways, and complex canal systems. It panicked populations, stymied the medical community, and caught governments unprepared to handle a health crisis. And most of all, it killed—hundreds of thousands in less than three years.

CHAPTER THREE

THE EPIDEMIC OF 1831-1834

֍

SO, AN EPIDEMIC ARRIVES . . . AND FINDS ITS PREY READY-MADE,

ITS VICTIMS HUDDLED TOGETHER AND WEAK.

—*Michel Chevalier, French economist, 1831*

N SEPTEMBER 1830 Lord Haytesbury, British ambassador to Russia, informed his government of a deadly disease that had infiltrated Russia's boundaries. "The accounts published by the [Russian] government of the ravages of this disease are . . . alarming," he wrote, "but those received by private correspondence are infinitely more so."

THE INVASION OF CHOLERA

When Haytesbury wrote his letter, cholera was sweeping through Russia. Moscow lost nearly half its population to the disease. Many Muscovites fled the city in panic—carrying

cholera with them to Saint Petersburg and Smolensk, among other towns.

From Russia cholera traveled along trade routes into Poland and the Baltic countries of northern Europe. Riga, a port city in this region, had a brisk overseas trade with England. In May of 1831, cholera struck Riga. From there, it jumped on board ship and made its way to England.

Cholera struck the port city of Sunderland in northern England in October 1831. A twelve-year-old girl named Isabella Hazard and a sailor named Sproate were the first to die. Within two months, cholera had spread throughout northeastern England. By February 1832, it had moved into London.

A sailor named Daniel Barber was the first victim of cholera in London. The physician who attended him at his deathbed described him as being in a "state of collapse, blue, cold and pulseless and suffering severely from spasms." Within

Cholera entered England via the port of Sunderland.

a week, two children, three women, and six men had followed Barber to the grave.

These deaths came in a cluster near Regent's Canal. Regent's Canal was linked to other canals and to the Thames River. The canals provided rich breeding grounds for cholera. The raw sewage and industrial waste pouring into them was, according to an 1831 report on sewer conditions, "so black that its course may be traced for many yards after it has mixed with the water of the Thames, which itself is not the purest of rivers."

The Thames and canals were the source of drinking water for many London neighborhoods. As wells became contaminated, many who drank from them became infected. Cholera spread like wildfire throughout London. Hundreds of people died swift, violent deaths in March and April.

The disease died out in London by the first week of May, only to resurface as the weather and water warmed in June. The epidemic peaked in the city during the summer months, then began to stalk other areas of the country.

Cholera traveled along the coastlines in the guts of people sailing aboard ships and in barrels of contaminated drinking water. It was carried inland with migrant laborers seeking work in mines and factory towns. By the end of September 1832, several regions in England, Scotland, and Ireland had succumbed to infection. Thousands sickened and hundreds died.

Meanwhile, other countries were suffering as well. Austria, Hungary, and Prussia were all hit in 1831–1832. France managed to stay clear of infection until the spring of 1832, when cholera traveled across the English Channel into France's port cities. From these ports, it quickly made its way to Paris.

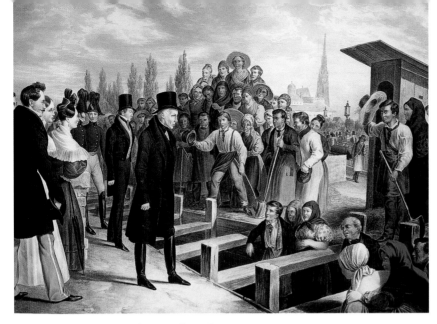

Franz I of Austria visits concerned citizens during the epidemic that broke out in his country in 1831.

As in other industrialized countries, France's cities were, in the words of one writer, filled with "ill-clad, ill-housed, and ill-fed people" and "narrow streets and dark, unhealthy buildings, as dank as dungeons, where those who toil come to catch their breath in fetid air." France's sewer and sanitation systems were likewise woefully insufficient. And although the country had a public health commission, this government body was totally unprepared to tackle a widespread outbreak of a little-known disease. As the government scrambled to control the situation, cholera raced through France's slums, killing more than 100,000 people, 18,000 in Paris alone, before it died out.

Across the Atlantic Ocean, citizens of Canada and the United States read newspaper reports about the cholera epidemics raging in Europe—and waited anxiously to see if their countries would be spared. For a few months, the ocean provided a natural barrier to the disease. Quarantine helped keep many infected people from entering North American ports.

Then, on May 31, 1832, a ship carrying emigrants from England landed in Quebec. The passengers on board were sick. Many had died on the overseas voyage. Those who were still healthy were desperate to leave the disease-ridden ship. They somehow dodged the quarantine and made it safely to

The Five Points slum forty years after the 1832 cholera epidemic.

land. Some of them carried the bacteria in their guts. Cholera had reached the New World.

Montreal reported the first case on June 6. Over the next few weeks, cholera swept through that city, then traveled down the Saint Lawrence River into New York State. It made several stops in small riverside villages before reaching New York City.

On June 26, an Irish immigrant named Fitzgerald fell ill with diarrhea and stomach cramps. He and his family lived in a filthy slum in New York City known as The Five Points. Fitzgerald survived his cholera infection, but his wife and two children, who came down with the same symptoms a few days later, did not. Cholera spread quickly through The Five Points, then moved on to the rest of New York City. The mortality count multiplied rapidly, until by the end of July more than a hundred cholera deaths a day were being reported.

New York City health officials were completely unprepared to handle the epidemic. Coffin makers could scarcely keep up with the orders. Death carts rattled to and fro on the streets. In some places, bodies lay rotting in gutters. Before the epidemic ended in August, more than 3,500 New Yorkers had died.

Meanwhile, cholera moved freely around the United States. By the end of 1832, states as far apart as Maine and Wisconsin reported cases of the disease. Most major cities were struck, including Baltimore, Philadelphia, and Detroit. Boston, Chicago, and Charleston escaped relatively unscathed, thanks to strict quarantine measures and better-than-average cleanliness. New Orleans, on the other hand,

CHOLERA *Curse of the Nineteenth Century*

proved to be very hospitable to cholera. It recorded five thousand deaths in less than two months in the fall of 1832.

Cholera continued to make appearances throughout 1833 and 1834. When it finally vanished at the end of 1834, the death toll for Canada and the United States was in the tens of thousands. In Europe, the toll was equally high. But worse perhaps than the death count was the effect cholera had on those who had witnessed and survived the epidemic. To many of these people, it was horrifyingly apparent that unless something was done to keep cholera at bay, the disease would continue to resurface and claim the lives of thousands more. But what action was to be taken against an enemy no one understood?

CONFRONTING AND COMBATING CHOLERA

Cholera is a disease born and raised in filth. In the industrialized cities of the nineteenth century, filth was most abundant in slums. The greatest number of cholera victims were the people who lived in those slums: the working-class poor.

This came as no surprise to the upper and middle classes. In fact, many believed the poor had brought the disease upon themselves because of immoral behavior and dirty habits. *"Drunkards and filthy, wicked people of all descriptions,* are swept away *in heaps* . . . just as we sweep away a mass of filth when it has become so corrupt that we cannot bear it" was a common attitude of those who believed God had sent cholera as punishment for sin.

In addition, most people still believed that disease was caused by poisonous clouds of foul air. One only had to walk the streets of a slum, where bodily odors combined with the stench of rotting garbage and raw sewage, to know that the air was fouler there than elsewhere.

Public sanitation workers hauled off waste and spread disinfectant.

While government officials shared the belief that filth and poverty caused cholera, they took a less accusatory approach to the problem than others. If they were to control the disease, they had to eradicate that which caused it. Therefore, they directed their attention to cleaning up the slums and helping the poor.

In many cities in different countries, massive efforts were made to remove decades of filth from the streets. Citizens were ordered to sweep their garbage into tidy piles that the sanitation department would then collect and remove. Sewers clogged with human waste were opened and cleaned out for the first time in many years. Ditches were dredged to allow better drainage. New water and sewer pipe systems were laid in some areas.

Unfortunately, these efforts to improve public hygiene usually led to trouble. For one thing, sanitation workers were not used to removing such a huge volume of garbage. Many simply refused to do so, while others demanded higher wages for the additional work. Those citizens who actually obeyed the order to gather their garbage were incensed when it lingered in stinking heaps outside their homes.

The improvements to the sewer systems, while noble in theory, often proved harmful in practice. Noxious fumes from open sewers drove many people from their homes and caused others to fear that a new miasma had been released. The raw sewage removed from pipes and ditches was collected in cesspools near the work sites, creating yet another place for cholera bacteria to live.

In addition to these problems, these projects were costly and time-consuming. A simpler and cheaper way to help the poor was to provide them with information that would help them help themselves.

In many cities, posters, handbills, and newspapers were printed that described cholera and how to prevent it. "Avoid crude [raw] vegetables and fruits; abstain . . . above all from ardent spirits [alcohol]," cautioned New York City newspapers. The poor were advised to wash themselves, their clothes, and their bedding regularly. Whitewashing the walls of their homes and dusting the interiors with lime would ward off the contagion, too, these publications stated.

Sewer construction projects were huge, filthy undertakings.

In addition to this information came practical help aimed at strengthening people's chances of fighting the disease. Soup kitchens doled out meals. Makeshift hospitals were organized to isolate victims. Many prosperous city dwellers donated money to charities that distributed it to the most needy.

Some members of the upper class also contributed their time. "Numbers of our most accomplished ladies are engaged day after day in making garments for the poor and distressed," announced one minister from New York, "while Committees of gentlemen . . . are searching out the abode of poverty, filth, and disease, and administering personally to the wants of the wretched inmates."

Many of these people acted out of an honest desire to help the poor, frequently ignoring the risk to their own health. Slum dwellers often had nowhere else to turn and so accepted the charity of the rich. But many were not happy doing so.

THE SUSPICIONS OF THE POOR

The working-class poor had long been suspicious of the upper classes. This mistrust was not unfounded. For years, the rich had all but ignored the plight of the poor. The sudden interest of the rich when cholera appeared deepened the poor's mistrust of them. They suspected that the upper classes were acting out of fear and self-preservation—in short, that they were trying to restrict the disease to the slums so that it wouldn't reach their own neighborhoods.

Many poor people refused to believe that cholera even existed. Instead, they whispered rumors that the upper classes were poisoning them as a way of decreasing their numbers and controlling those who survived. Such conspiracy theories circulated in the slums of many cities. The fear these rumors generated often led to riots and acts of violence. The upper classes of Paris, in particular, felt the wrath of the poor during this time.

No other segment of society came under greater suspicion than the medical profession. Hospitals in particular were greatly feared. They were filthy and overcrowded—and often the final resting place of those who entered them. (Many of the sick poor did not enter hospitals of their own free will but were forced into them by officials desperate to isolate them from the healthy.) Also, by the 1830s hospitals had become the primary source of cadavers. The bodies of the poor were increasingly used by doctors and students of anatomy for dissections. This practice horrified the families of the deceased, who wanted to give their loved ones proper burials—not have them cut up and studied.

"The common people firmly believe the doctors stupefy their patients with laudanum and then hurry them off to the grave while yet alive and that they have dissected living bodies," stated one observer. "Many well-informed people, too, think some have been interred alive."

When their fear of the medical community became too great, the poor reacted violently. Rioters threw stones at doctors, attacked hospitals, and refused to hand over the bodies of cholera victims. Doctors' houses and the homes of medical students were ransacked. Even those indirectly associated with the medical profession, such as the men who loaded and pulled the death carts and the charity workers who visited the sick, were refused entrance, forcibly turned out, and attacked. "I have never experienced any service so unpleasant as the present," wrote one Scottish doctor. "What between the hazard of the disease, the dangers of a lawless mob . . . I am extremely fatigued."

Doctors and the rich were not the only targets, however. Cholera, and fear of cholera, made the poor turn against each other as well. Sick neighbors were shunned. Coworkers looked upon one another with suspicion and fear. Even families collapsed. "The kindly affection of the father for his family is blunted or destroyed, the still stronger link of nature between the mother and her offspring is broken, and she looks on her innocent children as sources of danger," one person wrote in despair.

In general, the lives of the poor—already plagued by dangers both known and suspected—were shattered by the epidemic.

The Burke and Hare Murders

In the 1820s, the study of anatomy was on the rise. However, cadavers were so hard to come by that some doctors were willing to pay for whatever dead bodies they could get—no questions asked. Although the fee paid was not large, it was enough to entice some people into committing crimes such as grave robbing. And it was enough to turn two citizens of Edinburgh, Scotland, William Burke and William Hare, into the most notorious criminals of the era.

Burke and his mistress, Helen, lived in a boardinghouse that Hare ran along with his common-law wife, Margaret. In November 1827 another boarder, named Donald, died owing Hare rent money. Enraged, Hare decided to sell Donald's body to get the money owed to him. He brought Burke, a man always ready to make a fast buck, into his plan. Together they removed Donald's body from its coffin and substituted tree bark in its place. Then they bundled up the body and brought it, as previously arranged, to Dr. Robert Knox.

Dr. Knox was a professor of surgery and anatomy. He paid handsomely for Donald. Excited by this easy money, Burke and Hare determined to acquire more bodies—by any means necessary.

William Burke

They got their chance several days later. Another boarder, Joseph, was sick. Pretending to be concerned, Burke and Hare gave Joseph a glass of whiskey—and then another, and another, until Joseph was so drunk he passed out. Burke and Hare seized their opportunity. One held Joseph's nose and mouth closed while the other held him down until Joseph died of suffocation—and Burke and Hare had another body to deliver to Dr. Knox.

Over the next ten months, Burke and Hare killed at least sixteen people, including a grandmother and her deaf grandson, a mother and a daughter, and a relative of Helen's. Helen and Margaret knew of the murders and sometimes helped find the victims. Dr. Knox paid for each body—no questions asked.

In the beginning, Burke and Hare chose only those people they figured no one would miss. But toward the end, they made the mistake of killing a well-known figure in the neighborhood known as Daft Jamie. Several of Knox's anatomy students becognized Jamie during his dissection. Although many wondered how Jamie came to be on the anatomy table, no one went so far as to accuse Dr. Knox of purchasing a murder victim.

Then, on Halloween night, 1828, Burke and Hare were finally found out. The day before, they had killed a woman named Mary Docherty and stashed her body under a bed. Two boarders discovered the body. Horrified, they called the police.

Burke, Hare, Helen, and Margaret were arrested soon after. However, since no one had witnessed the actual murders, the prosecutors had a hard time making a case against them. So they offered Hare and Margaret immunity in exchange for their testimony against Burke and Helen. Hare and Margaret jumped at the chance.

On Christmas Day, 1828, William Burke was found guilty of murdering sixteen people. He was executed on January 28, 1829. For lack of evidence, Helen was found not guilty. She disappeared from Edinburgh shortly after her release. Hare and Margaret were released in February 1829. They, too, left Edinburgh, although by most reports not together. Dr. Knox was never tried for his part in the crimes, but he was completely discredited and shunned in Edinburgh. He moved to London, where he worked in a cancer hospital until his death in 1862.

William Hare

Burke and Hare's violent crime spree left an indelible mark on the medical profession. The murders had been done to supply bodies for dissection—therefore, the medical profession was at least partly to blame. In addition, the murders only increased people's fear and suspicion of doctors in general, and anatomists and surgeons in particular—for how could they trust anyone who might have paid for the bodies of their friends, coworkers, or even family members?

The murders left a mark on the English language as well. The term *to burke* means "to suppress something quietly," and comes, of course, from the way Burke had killed his victims—by smothering. Several plays and movies have been made about the murders, and this macabre verse was sung by schoolchildren for decades after:

Up the close and down the stair,
In the house with Burke and Hare.
Burke's the butcher, Hare's the thief,
And Knox the boy who buys the beef.

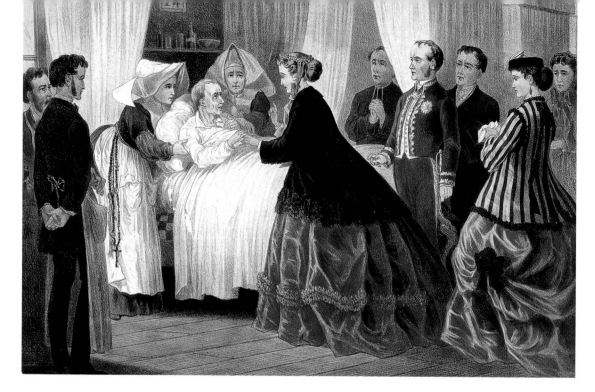

Even the wealthy fell victim to cholera.

CHOLERA AND THE RICH

Rich people became infected with cholera just as readily as the poor. However, the rich were more likely to survive because they had access to cleaner drinking water, better sanitation, and superior living conditions. Such advantages meant they didn't suffer from repeated exposure to the cholera bacteria. In fact, cholera posed a greater threat to their wealth than to their health.

As has been mentioned, many rich people showed their empathy for the poor by doing charitable work. But many others chose to cut themselves off from the diseased poor by shutting themselves up in their houses or leaving town. "The roads, in all directions, were lined with well-filled stage coaches, livery coaches, private vehicles and equestrians, all panic struck, fleeing the city," reported one New York newspaper.

Those who fled left behind empty mansions and closed shops filled with expensive items. These places became prime targets for burglars and looters. "The cases of housebreaking are numerous, and the plunderers of private dwellings . . .

destroy what they cannot carry away. Carpets are cut to pieces and furniture broken to pieces by these wretches," the paper lamented.

Law enforcement officials in most cities were hard-pressed to prevent such theft and vandalism because they were so busy trying to stem the tide of the epidemic. Many were struggling to enforce quarantines that businessmen were struggling just as hard to remove.

"The mercantile and shipping interests of this port, dreading that restriction might be imposed upon the commerce, are strongly opposed to the belief that cholera exists here," wrote one official about a conspiracy to cover up the cholera outbreak in Sunderland, England.

Many businessmen suspected that those who ordered the quarantines—doctors and local boards of health—were exaggerating cholera's importance in order to strengthen their own positions. "Cases of cholera have been made out of toothache, stabbing in the abdomen with a fork, jaundice, dropsy and every complaint in the vocabulary of the disease," accused one merchant.

Such accusations did much to discredit the struggling medical profession. Had doctors been able to come up with a cause and cure for cholera, they would undoubtedly have been celebrated as miracle workers. Instead, their inability to find a solution to the problem—indeed their inability to reach a consensus about the disease within their own ranks—made them appear weak and ineffectual.

CURING CHOLERA

When it came to fighting cholera, most European and American doctors were working in the dark. Few had ever witnessed the disease; those who saw it for the first time were horrified at how it killed its victims. There were plenty of doctors who, like the wealthy, chose to flee in the face of cholera rather than fight it.

Those who stayed to fight differed in their interpretation of the disease. Some doctors believed that cholera attacked with varying levels of severity. How severe the attack was depended upon a person's behavior. Those who ate sparingly, abstained from alcohol, and remained calm were less vulnerable. On the other hand, those who allowed their bodies to become susceptible by showing strong emotion or indulging themselves in food and drink ran a greater risk of severe illness or death. Doctors who subscribed to this belief usually felt that faith in God and obedience to his lessons—that a person should be temperate, avoid gluttony, and keep his or her emotions in check—were the surest means of preventing cholera attacks.

In an attempt to cure the disease, doctors tried various treatments. Some relied on age-old practices, such as bloodletting. Others advised high doses of the laxative calomel, a chalky form of the metal mercury. Still others prescribed narcotics such as laudanum. All of these treatments could be dangerous.

Doctors sometimes tried to combat only the symptoms of the disease. To stop uncontrollable diarrhea, they recommended plugging the rectum with such substances as beeswax or oilskin. To help cold, clammy skin become warm and dry, they advised rubbing the patient with cayenne pepper, chalk, or mercury ointment. Clearly, these methods were doomed to fail.

You can't be too careful! An 1831 German illustration pokes fun at the lengths people would go to ward off cholera. This fellow is "armed" with branches of herbs and wears a "protective" suit—part rubber, part copper, part fabric.

CHOLERA *Curse of the Nineteenth Century*

There was one treatment that might have helped, had it not been just as likely to kill the patient: an injection of a saline solution, a mixture of water and salt, into the bloodstream. The treatment was similar to what modern medicine would prescribe for cholera victims. In 1832, however, physicians were unskilled at administering injections. They sometimes introduced a life-threatening air bubble into a patient's bloodstream. Or, as a result of dirty hands and instruments, they infected the victim at the site of the injection.

Doctors were still struggling to discover the cause of cholera when the epidemic died out in 1834. The disease had killed hundreds of thousands throughout Europe, the United States, and Canada, many of them poor city dwellers. Cholera had made people realize that the very things they were proudest of—their flourishing industries and cities—had nearly been the cause of their downfall.

Unfortunately, the lessons people might have learned from this deadly epidemic did not sink in. Years later, when cholera struck again, very little had been done to improve sanitation, drinking water, or public health. If anything, cholera found conditions even better for its survival than it had the first time it attacked.

LE CHOLÉRA

CHAPTER FOUR

CHOLERA STRIKES AGAIN

ᘈᘕᘈ

ANOTHER SPRING WILL BRING CHOLERA AMONG US,
SWEEPING LIKE THE ANGEL OF DEATH OVER OUR FIRESIDES.
—Weekly Wisconsin *newspaper, December 27, 1848*

 T WOULD BE SEVERAL YEARS before cholera returned to Europe and North America—years during which people and governments could have worked to improve the conditions of their cities and prevent another serious outbreak. However, as one person noted in an 1845 report, "no sooner had the impressive period of danger passed . . . than the drainage and cleansing were neglected as before."

Although some countries, England most notably, took a long, hard look at their sanitary conditions, public health reforms that had seemed so crucial in 1832 didn't seem quite as necessary once the threat of cholera had passed. Boards of health that had been formed during the epidemic were dis-

Opposite:
Cholera struck again and again in the nineteenth century. This illustration, which appeared on the cover of a French magazine, portrays the disease as an indiscriminate killer, cutting down all in its path.

banded or, if they stayed together, were typically understaffed and ineffective. Aid to the poor dwindled, and tax money was spent on things other than improving sewers and cleaning up water supplies. Meanwhile urban populations continued to grow. And people were moving around more than ever before, from city to city, from country to country. If anything, the conditions that had allowed cholera to take root in 1832 were even worse sixteen years later, when cholera returned, with a vengeance, to the industrialized world.

THE PANDEMICS OF 1839 AND 1854

The third worldwide outbreak of cholera followed much the same route as the first two pandemics. It began with an epidemic in India in 1839. From there the disease made its way into Russia, where it killed thousands. By 1848 Europe was besieged; no country on the continent escaped infection.

In Britain, the dead totaled close to 61,000—almost double the number killed in the 1831 epidemic. France recorded a sobering 104,000 deaths. Italy's dead numbered about 24,000.

In December 1848, a ship carrying Irish immigrants dropped anchor in New York City's harbor. Seven people on board were dead from cholera already. The ship was placed under quarantine, and many more died. Some terrified passengers slipped through the quarantine to escape death. Many of those who reached shore brought cholera with them.

In the following months, people traveling aboard trains, in wagons, and on riverboats spread the disease in the United States. In addition, the lure of gold and the prospect of cheap land had encouraged many Easterners to uproot themselves and seek a new life in the territories of the West. Cholera

Travelers in the United States wait for a train to take them—and the cholera bacteria they may carry—to new places.

journeyed with them, claiming the lives of many pioneers and gold seekers.

Some U.S. cities lost up to one-tenth of their populations. New York recorded more than five thousand deaths in four months. Places that had escaped the disease the first time around, such as Chicago and Boston, found they were no longer immune.

The epidemic subsided by the end of 1849, and few cases were reported for five years. Then, from 1854 to 1855, cholera once again reared its head, striking across the globe and killing hundreds of thousands of people before finally dying out.

Throughout the pandemics of 1839 and 1854, most people continued to believe that the root of the disease was the immoral behavior and filthy habits of the working-class poor. Many preached that the poor had brought the disease upon themselves.

Many, but not all. Since the first cholera outbreak in 1831, a politician, a statistician, and a doctor in England had been working independently to formulate different theories of how the disease and poverty were connected.

EDWIN CHADWICK

Sir Edwin Chadwick, pioneer for social reform

In 1837, a liberal-minded politician named Edwin Chadwick (1800–1890) was commissioned by Parliament to study the state of sanitation in the poorer sections of England. The goal of his research was to determine if changes to the Poor Laws—laws that governed how aid was distributed to the poor—were needed. Over the next five years, he made many visits to the slums to research his subject personally. In 1842, he published his findings in a three-hundred-page report entitled *The Sanitary Conditions of the Labouring Population of Great Britain.* Seven thousand copies of the report were printed.

Chadwick's report horrified most people who read it. Page after page cited explicit examples of the appalling sanitary conditions with which the poor were forced to live. Chadwick also presented a model for a self-perpetuating cycle of poverty and disease. In essence, he claimed that poverty led to unsanitary conditions, which led to sickness. A sick person couldn't work and might lose his or her job—a situation that led to increased poverty and back to the beginning of the cycle.

Chadwick supported his model with statistics that showed that the working classes were much more susceptible to disease and more likely to die at an early age than the upper classes. He placed the blame for this inequality on poor sanitation and sewer systems, lack of clean water supplies, and accumulations of refuse—not, like many of his contemporaries, on the habits of the poor people themselves. He called upon Parliament to step forward and reform the laws that governed sanitation and public health.

Chadwick's report created a great public outcry and a frenzy of political debate. Many took Chadwick's side and lobbied for the government to assume control of public sanitation and health. Others continued to argue that sanitation was a matter for individuals or local authorities to pay for and deal with, not the central government.

In the end, Chadwick and his supporters won. In August 1848, Parliament passed the Public Health Act; a month later the Nuisance Removal Act was approved. These acts put the responsibility for providing adequate sanitation, refuse removal, clean water, and proper ventilation of buildings in the hands of the central government for the first time.

Chadwick's cause was undoubtedly helped by the fact that cholera was raging in continental Europe in 1848. People in England feared that unless sanitary reforms were passed, it would strike their country again. Unfortunately, the Acts were too late to prevent the disease's spread. Still, Chadwick's report and campaign had opened many people's eyes to the public health problems faced by the poor.

WILLIAM FARR

William Farr (1807–1883) was the superintendent of the General Register Office. During his forty-year career, he compiled huge volumes of statistics about the people of England, including births, marriages, and deaths.

Throughout the 1848–1849 cholera epidemic, Farr gathered information about people who died of the disease, including the address, economic status, sex, and age of victims. He hoped the data would allow people to predict where cholera was likely to strike in the future.

Using his statistics, Farr plotted the course of cholera's

spread through the English population during the 1848 epidemic. When he examined the data for London, he discovered something interesting. Neighborhoods closest to the Thames had higher death rates than those farther away. In addition, he realized that areas of high elevation with good drainage suffered less than low-lying areas with poor drainage.

From this evidence, Farr deduced that the Thames was somehow connected to the spread of cholera. But, like most of his learned contemporaries, he believed in the miasma theory of disease. He could readily believe that a poisonous, cholera-laden cloud had formed over the stinking Thames and delivered the disease to those unfortunate enough to live near the river. The conclusion that the water of the Thames itself was the culprit eluded him. It would take a doctor with a special interest in cholera to make that important connection.

DR. JOHN SNOW

John Snow (1813–1858) was an anesthesiologist by profession. His skill at administering ether and chloroform to surgical patients and women in labor brought him recognition during his lifetime. But it was his study of cholera that earned him a place in today's history books.

During his medical training in London, Snow saw and treated many victims of cholera. The disease intrigued him; he especially wanted to unravel the mystery of how it was contracted. He noted that, unlike other epidemic illnesses such as smallpox that caused high fever, rashes, or respiratory problems, cholera attacked the stomach and the intestines, leading to diarrhea and vomiting. Therefore, Snow concluded, "the morbid material producing cholera must . . . be swallowed accidentally, for persons would not take it intentionally; and the increase of the morbid material, or cholera poison, must take place in the interior of the stomach and bowels."

In other words, cholera was caused by something the victim had either eaten or drunk. And if this were true, then all cholera victims had to have consumed the same thing. The key was to discover what that thing was and where they got it.

At some point during his inquiry into cholera, Snow became familiar with the reports made by Chadwick and Farr. Snow saw connections the other two men had missed. Snow knew from Chadwick's report—and his own observations, undoubtedly—that the Thames River was polluted. Farr's study had shown that people who lived close to the Thames in low-lying areas with poor drainage were more likely to die than those who lived farther away, on higher ground that was well drained.

Then Snow made a historic jump: if people were ingesting something that caused cholera, then that something could originate in the filthy water of the Thames—the water that Londoners were drinking.

In 1849, Snow published a pamphlet, *On the Mode of Communication of Cholera*, that outlined his hypothesis that cholera was a water-borne disease. However, his idea flew in the face of the commonly held miasma theory and so was dismissed by most in the medical community. And as the 1848 cholera epidemic had subsided by that time, Snow had no way of proving his theory.

THE BROAD STREET PUMP

Then, in the summer of 1854, cholera returned to London. As the number of sick and dead mounted, Snow decided to put his theory to the test. He chose the London neighborhood of Broad Street, where cholera was striking with particular ferocity.

Dr. John Snow traced the 1854 cholera outbreak to a community pump such as this.

Snow sketched out a map of Broad Street and the surrounding areas. On it he included the points where people had sickened or died of cholera. He also indicated where public water supplies were located. When it was finished, his map showed that a cluster of deaths had occurred within a few hundred yards of one particular water source, the Broad Street pump.

Snow paid a visit to the site. After seeing the dirty water that flowed from the pump, he became more convinced than ever that the water drawn from the Broad Street supply was causing the deaths. The only way to stop more people from dying, he believed, was to prevent them from drinking the water.

On September 7, 1854, Snow asked local authorities to remove the handle from the pump so that people could no longer draw water. His request was granted immediately. In only a few days, there were fewer cholera cases, and then there were none. Removing the handle had ended the epidemic, at least for the people of the Broad Street neighborhood. Snow had proven his theory—and, equally important, he had saved lives.

In 1855, Snow published an expanded version of his 1849 pamphlet on cholera. He presented a great deal of evidence supporting his conclusion that cholera was bred and spread through contaminated water, including instances in which cholera cases had ceased when other doctors had shut off filthy water supplies. Yet despite this evidence, the medical community did not readily accept Snow's water-borne theory over that of miasma. Not even Chadwick and Farr, whose research had contributed to the formation of Snow's conclusions, supported Snow at first.

In time, however, Snow's theory gained momentum—and when the next cholera epidemic swept through Europe and North America, many cities were better prepared to combat the disease and stem its spread.

CHAPTER FIVE

BEYOND THE BROAD STREET PUMP

∽◦∾

BOIL IT, COOK IT, PEEL IT, OR FORGET IT.
—a current guide to travelers for the prevention of cholera,
from the Centers for Disease Control, Atlanta, Georgia

HEN CHOLERA RETURNED TO EUROPE IN 1865, it found some cities less hospitable than in previous visits. London, in particular, had moved forward. England's largest city had worked at improving sewer systems, cleaning up drinking water supplies, and collecting and disposing of refuse.

The efforts paid off. When cholera reached the city's shores, a few months after striking western Europe, it no longer leaked from the Thames into wells and other water supplies. The Thames itself was looking and smelling cleaner than it had for generations. Although the epidemic still killed several thousand people during its stay in London, its spread

Opposite:

A construction crew at work on London's new sewer system, 1859

49

Corporate Cover-Up

During the 1866 cholera epidemic in London, one section of the city, East London, recorded an abnormally high number of cases and deaths. Of the 4,363 estimated deaths that occurred in the city between July 1 and September 1, more than 3,700 happened in this section.

The situation caught the attention of William Farr. Upon investigation, he discovered that the people who died had received their water from the East London Water Company. Snow's theory loomed large before him.

When Farr paid a visit to the company, he was assured that the East London water supply was completely separate from its sewage and that the water underwent filtration before reaching consumers. Not satisfied, Farr dug a little deeper. He soon found two East London customers who claimed they had recently discovered eels in their water pipes—something that couldn't have happened if the water had indeed been properly filtered.

Then Farr heard from Joseph Bazalgette. For the past six years, Bazalgette had been constructing sewer systems to divert sewage away from waterways that led to the Thames. Bazalgette had made all the necessary diversions except for those in the East London area. He immediately set up a temporary diversion there.

Joseph Bazalgette

Once Bazalgette's diversion was in place, the number of cholera cases among those served by the East London company dropped. Although the East London Water Company was never held accountable for the problems it had caused, one positive thing did emerge from the incident. Farr finally found himself agreeing with Snow's theory that cholera was a water-borne disease.

Snow, unfortunately, would never know of Farr's conversion, for he had died in 1858. The exact cause of his death is not known, but modern historians speculate that he may have suffered a stroke brought on by years of self-experimentation with ether and chloroform.

was limited once sources of contamination were discovered.

Changes were also occurring in the United States, most notably in New York City. On February 26, 1866, just prior to the spring outbreak of cholera, the New York State legislature established a permanent board of health. The Metropolitan Board of Health was responsible for generating and implementing plans to clean the city's streets, maintain the safety of the water supply, and promote good public hygiene. It also devised a specific plan to stop cholera if and when it invaded New York City again.

The board based its plan on a unanimously approved statement issued by the New York Academy of Medicine. The academy's doctors agreed that "the cholera diarrhoea and 'rice-water discharges' . . . are capable . . . of propagating [spreading] the cholera poison" and that "rigidly enforced precautions should be taken in every case of cholera to permanently disinfect or destroy those ejected fluids." In other words, when a case of cholera appeared, people should do all they could to clean the infected home while avoiding contact with the victim's excrement or vomit.

On May 1, 1866, the first new cholera case in New York City was reported, and the Metropolitan Board of Health was forced to put its plan into action. The victim's living quarters were scoured clean and spread with lime to disinfect them. His clothing, bedding, and utensils were removed and burned. Other residents in the building were moved to a hospital.

As additional cholera cases popped up in various parts of the city, the board took the same actions. Fortunately, the plan worked. Compared to the five thousand deaths reported in the last epidemic, New York City counted only five hundred in 1866.

Proof of the plan's effectiveness also came in the form of comparisons with death rates in cities that had no board of health or cholera plan. Cincinnati, for example, recorded more than 1,200 deaths. Saint Louis lost nearly triple that number of people.

Yet even as effective means of combating and controlling cholera were implemented, one vital piece of knowledge about the disease continued to elude doctors and scientists. What caused it? By this time there was plenty of evidence to show that something in polluted water was to blame, but no one knew what it was. Not until 1883, when a German scientist named Robert Koch reported isolating *V. cholerae* under his microscope, would researchers get their first glimpse of the culprit.

DR. ROBERT KOCH

Robert Koch (1843–1910) has a place in history as one of the founders of bacteriology, the study of bacteria. His experiments helped prove to the world that specific microbes caused specific diseases.

Koch was born in Germany. While in high school he became interested in biology. Upon graduation he entered the University of Göttingen, where he first studied natural science and then medicine. One of his professors was a pathologist who taught that disease was caused by microorganisms that infected the body; these teachings greatly influenced Koch's later work. After graduating with a medical degree in 1866, he worked as a general practitioner until 1870, when he joined the army to fight in the Franco-Prussian War (1870–1871). In 1872, Koch turned from general practice to begin his study of disease-causing bacteria.

When Koch first studied bacteria, he was hindered by the

fact that the microbes he wanted to study didn't stand out from the material that surrounded them. He solved the problem by developing a method of staining the bacteria with dye. Suddenly, a teeming world of microorganisms materialized beneath his microscope.

Robert Koch performs experiments in his laboratory.

In 1877 Koch published four requirements for proving that a specific microbe was the cause of a certain disease. The first stated that the microbe suspected of causing a disease had to be found in samples taken from every subject who had the disease. The second said that several generations of that same microbe had to be reproduced in a pure culture in a laboratory. Thirdly, microbes from one of these later generations had to cause the same disease when injected into experimental animals. And lastly, the same microbe had to be recovered from samples taken from the experimental animals. These requirements became known as Koch's postulates. They soon became the basis for studying disease-causing bacteria. (Researchers still follow the same general guidelines today.)

Koch put his postulates and bacteria-staining methods to good use. In 1882, he isolated and identified the bacterium that causes tuberculosis, an endeavor that later earned him the Nobel Prize. In 1883, two years after the sixth pandemic had begun its deadly course, he turned his attention to cholera and began to hunt for the bacterium that caused the disease.

Unknown to Koch, an Italian scientist named Filippo Pacini (1812–1883) had conducted similar research thirty years earlier. In 1854, Pacini isolated a unique microorganism in the feces of cholera victims. He identified the organism as a vibrio, a comma-shaped bacterium that moves by thrashing a tail, and linked it to cholera. But unfortunately for Pacini—and for thousands of cholera sufferers—no one took note of his discovery. It was only in 1965 that Pacini's research came to light and the Italian scientist was given his rightful place in medical history as the discoverer of *V. cholerae.*

When Koch began his investigations into cholera in 1883, Egypt and India were still suffering its effects. The German government sent Koch to Cairo to study the disease. When the epidemic subsided there, he moved on to India to continue his research.

Koch and his team of assistants analyzed samples of drinking water and food from areas where cholera was running out of control. They examined fecal matter from cholera victims. When the same comma-shaped bacterium was found in all samples, Koch was sure he had discovered the microbe responsible for cholera. Further experiments proved him correct.

Now that Koch had the culprit in hand, he was determined to put an end to its crime spree. The epidemic that had brought him to Egypt and India had spread to China and Japan in the Far East and into the port cities of Toulon and Marseille in France. From France it traveled to Italy, where it killed seven thousand in Naples alone.

By the time cholera reached western Europe, Koch had already returned to Germany. He helped the German government develop methods of checking and filtering water supplies and sewage to ensure they were free of the deadly bacteria. In time, these methods helped Germany put a stop to the epidemic. When other countries adopted the same methods, the outbreak slowly but surely began to subside in Europe.

Not in time, however, to prevent it from crossing the ocean to America. But when cholera struck the port of New York in 1892, the city was ready. It quickly implemented its plan to control the outbreak and snuffed out the disease before it could spread throughout the country.

Today, Europe and North America stay virtually cholera free, thanks to the constant filtration and chlorination of water supplies and sophisticated sanitation and sewer systems. Sadly, not all countries in the world have access to these technologies. They remain vulnerable to outbreaks of cholera, as well as other diseases.

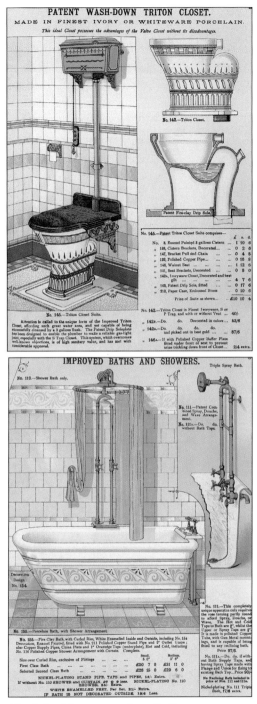

The latest in personal sanitation products, c. 1890

CHOLERA TODAY

The seventh pandemic of cholera started in 1961 and continues to strike today. Unlike previous pandemics that trace their origins back to India, the 1961 pandemic began in Indonesia. It was caused by a new strain of *V. cholerae,* which researchers named El Tor. El Tor swarmed through Asia in the 1960s. In 1970, it turned up in West Africa, where it's been endemic ever since. By 1991 it had made it to Peru.

Three separate ports in this South American country reported cases within days of each other. Although researchers, scientists, and doctors scrambled to control the disease, El Tor quickly made its way through Peru and into other countries in Latin America. As time went by, hundreds of thousands of cases were reported, and death counts mounted into the thousands.

Why, when so much was understood about the disease, was cholera able to make such headway? Part of the reason was that Peru and its neighbors were experiencing the same sort of conditions that had been present in Europe during the nineteenth century. The population of Peruvian towns had grown rapidly, while the sanitation and sewerage systems lagged behind. Water supplies were not properly filtrated or chlorinated.

Cholera was communicated not just through water but food as well. Vegetables, seafood, rice, and other products, typically sold in open marketplaces, were contaminated with bacteria. If they were not properly washed, cooked, or handled, they carried disease to anyone who ate them.

And finally, South America, like Europe in the previous century, had improved systems of transportation. *V. cholerae* took advantage, traveling with ease from country to country in the guts of infected people.

Cholera's means of transmission was fairly obvious. South

America, however, had been free of cholera for decades. So the question on the minds of most scientists was, how had the bacteria reached Peru in the first place? The answer to that question came as a result of years of research by one U.S. scientist.

DR. RITA COLWELL

Microbiologist and current head of the National Science Foundation, Dr. Rita Colwell began studying cholera in 1969. Colwell's first breakthrough came in the 1970s. She showed that *V. cholerae* goes into a dormant state unless conditions are just right. The bacterium is still alive, but it can't replicate. No scientist had considered this possibility before. The common belief was that when the bacterium ran out of humans to infect, it died. Colwell's studies proved otherwise.

Furthermore, Colwell discovered that cholera bacteria favor warm water with a high sodium chloride content—ocean water in tropical climates, in other words. The bacteria go into the dormant state when water temperatures are cold. However, dormant cholera bacteria are still capable of causing infection if ingested, as Colwell proved by injecting volunteers with such bacteria and recording their subsequent infections.

Colwell's studies showed once again how vital proper filtration and chlorination systems are to preventing cholera outbreaks. The dormant bacteria she and her team discovered had come from water samples from Chesapeake Bay, off Maryland and Virginia, and a bayou close to the city of New Orleans in Louisiana. Although the bacteria existed in these waters, filtration and chlorination had kept them from reaching water supplies in the United States.

Recently, Colwell made another, equally significant discovery about *V. cholerae*. She discovered that cholera bacteria are parasitic, that is, they live off other organisms. While in the ocean, cholera bacteria attach themselves to microscopic water animals known as zooplankton. Their favorite zooplankton seems to be the copepod. Copepods feed on phytoplankton, microscopic water plants. When water temperatures rise, these plants often undergo a population explosion known as an algal bloom. The animals that feed on the plants grow in number right along with the plants—and when they do, the cholera bacteria suddenly have a vast new supply of hosts. Therefore, when water temperatures increase, the likelihood of cholera outbreaks rises.

Copepods float in ocean water, traveling with the currents, washing up with tides, and entering estuaries. When the copepods and their parasites reach an area where the drinking water isn't filtered or chlorinated, the water becomes contaminated. Colwell, and other scientists as well, think that just such a series of events may have led to the 1991 epidemic in Peru.

Rita Colwell's contribution to the body of cholera knowledge has helped the medical community keep a closer eye on *V. cholerae*. Her work has spurred researchers to begin developing methods of predicting where and when cholera might strike. If one day scientists can predict cholera outbreaks, as they do hurricanes, the entire world will be a safer place.

CHOLERA'S LEGACY— AND FUTURE

HOLERA IS BORN IN AND SPREAD THROUGH FILTH. This was the lesson the pandemics of the nineteenth century taught the Western world. It was a lesson that was slow to sink in—but when it did, it generated a movement to improve public health that might otherwise have been postponed for years to come.

In the wake of cholera, governments of western Europe and North America undertook massive public works projects, created and expanded sewer systems, introduced water filtration and chlorination, and in general made the cleanliness of their cities and towns of utmost importance. Cholera's legacy lives on in the sanitation systems, water departments,

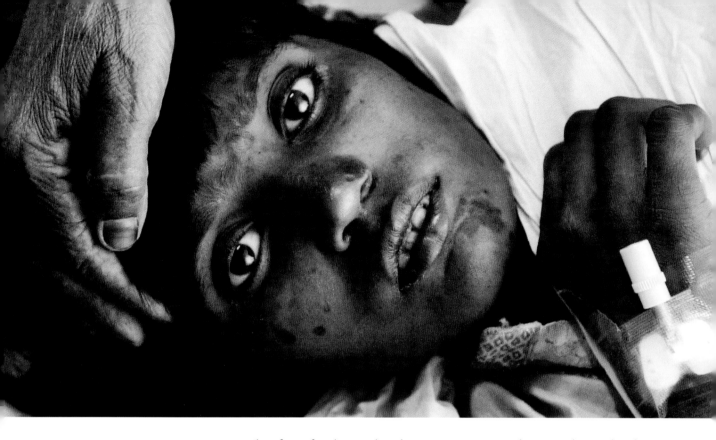

and refuse facilities that keep our streets clean and our drinking water safe.

This legacy has not found its way into all parts of the world, however. The official Web site of the World Health Organization (WHO) contains details of recent disease outbreaks, including outbreaks of cholera. The majority of cases occur in African countries such as Liberia, Malawi, Burundi, Niger, and Congo. As many as 22,000 individuals become infected each year in these countries, with deaths numbering in the hundreds.

WHO and other humanitarian associations are working hard to raise money to help these countries build the necessary facilities to keep cholera at bay, but so far their efforts have fallen short. Until they are successful, or some other means of keeping the bacteria from reaching drinking supplies is implemented, the disease will likely continue to recur—and another chapter in the history of cholera will be written.

TIME LINE OF CHOLERA EVENTS

1817: First cholera pandemic begins in India

1826: Second cholera pandemic begins in India

1830: Cholera reaches Europe for the first time

1832: Cholera reaches the United States and Canada for the first time

1839: Third cholera pandemic begins in India

1847: Cholera strikes Europe again

1848: Cholera reaches the United States and Canada again

1849: Dr. John Snow publishes first treatise *On the Mode of Communication of Cholera*

1854: Fourth cholera pandemic strikes Europe, United States, and Canada; pump handle removed from Broad Street pump at Snow's request, and cholera cases cease in Broad Street neighborhood; Filippo Pacini identifies a microorganism in the feces of cholera victims, but his discovery goes unnoticed by most of the medical world

1855: Snow publishes expanded treatise *On the Mode of Communication of Cholera*

1863: Fifth cholera pandemic begins in India

1865: Cholera reaches western Europe

1866: Cholera reaches North America

1881: Sixth cholera pandemic begins in India

1883: Dr. Robert Koch isolates and identifies the bacterium that causes cholera; receives credit as the discoverer of *V. cholerae*

1891: Cholera strikes France, Italy, and Germany

1892: Cholera strikes North America, but is quickly controlled

1961: Seventh cholera pandemic begins in Indonesia

1991: Cholera strikes Peru, spreads throughout South America

GLOSSARY

anatomy the structure of a living body and all its parts; the scientific field of studying the human body, its parts, and how those parts fit together and work

anesthesia a drug given to create the partial or complete loss of sensitivity to pain, usually administered prior to a surgical operation or painful procedure

antiseptics chemicals used to remove germs and bacteria in order to create a sterile, infection-free environment

bacteria single-celled microorganisms, some of which cause disease (singular: bacterium)

cadaver a dead body, especially one intended for dissection

endemic disease a disease that is always present at low levels in a society

epidemic an outbreak of a disease that affects a large number of people in a particular region

estuary the mouth of a river where its current meets the ocean and is affected by the tides; freshwater and salt water mingle in an estuary

excrement solid bodily waste

excrete to eliminate waste from the body

feces solid bodily waste

laudanum a solution containing opium, once commonly prescribed by doctors for various ailments

miasma a poisonous cloud of foul-smelling air that was once thought to cause illness

microbe a very tiny living thing; a microorganism

pandemic an outbreak of a disease that affects a great number of people worldwide at about the same time

paralysis a condition in which the body or parts of the body cannot move

quarantine a period of time during which ships, people, animals, or objects are isolated until they are determined to be free of disease

replicate to duplicate or reproduce

sanitation the protection of people's health by keeping living conditions clean

secrete to produce and release a chemical substance into the body

toxin a poisonous substance produced by living organisms such as bacteria

TO FIND OUT MORE

BOOKS

Hayhurst, Chris. *Cholera (Epidemics): Deadly Diseases Throughout History.* New York: Rosen Publishing Group, 2001.
   Written for middle-grade readers, this book gives some history of the disease but focuses more on the current state of understanding and controlling cholera.

Hoff, Brent, and Carter Smith III. *Mapping Epidemics: A Historical Atlas of Disease.* New York: Franklin Watts, 2000.
   An interesting book with maps and text that describe the spread of many infectious diseases, including cholera.

Wilkinson, Philip, and Michael Pollard. *Ideas That Changed the World: The Industrial Revolution.* New York: Chelsea House Publishers, 1995.
   A middle-grade reader that highlights the inventions and advancements of the Industrial Revolution.

ON THE INTERNET*

"Snow on Cholera" at

www.ph.ucla.edu/epi/snow.html

An in-depth history of the contributions made by Dr. John Snow and William Farr. Includes biographies of the two men, the complete text of Snow's publication *On the Mode of Communication of Cholera*, maps of the Broad Street pump neighborhood, and quotes by Snow's contemporaries.

"Robert Koch" at

http://web.ukonline.co.uk/b.gardner/Koch.htm

Biography of Dr. Robert Koch, including his four postulates.

"Tracking a Killer: Following Cholera with Every Available Means" at

www.nsf.gov/od/lpa/news/publicat/frontier/10-96/10chlra.htm

An article published by *Frontiers*, the official newsletter of the National Science Foundation, on the recent discoveries about cholera. Includes information on Dr. Rita Colwell, director of the foundation.

"Cholera Returns" at

www.wri.org/wri/wr-98-99/cholera.htm

An article published by the World Resources Institute of Washington, D.C., outlining the link between the environment, climate, and cholera.

"The Crime Library: Burke and Hare" at

www.crimelibrary.com/serial9/burke-hare

Tells the gruesome story of the 1828 murders.

"The History of Plumbing" at

www.theplumber.com

Gives a detailed account of the history of plumbing, from ancient through modern times, and includes links to biographies of those who contributed to plumbing, such as Thomas Crapper.

*All Internet sites were available and accurate when this book was sent to press.

BIBLIOGRAPHY

Bray, R. S. *Armies of Pestilence: The Impact of Disease on History.* New York: Barnes and Noble Books, 1996.

Clare, John D., ed. *Industrial Revolution.* San Diego: Harcourt Brace and Company, 1994.

Delaporte, Francois. *Disease and Civilization: The Cholera in Paris, 1832.* Cambridge, MA: The MIT Press, 1986.

Durey, Michael. *The Return of the Plague: British Society and the Cholera 1831–1832.* Dublin: Gill and Macmillan, 1979.

Editors of Time-Life Books. *What Life Was Like in Europe's Romantic Era.* Alexandria, VA: Time Inc., 2000.

Hayhurst, Chris. *Cholera (Epidemics): Deadly Diseases Throughout History.* New York: Rosen Publishing Group, 2001.

Hoff, Brent, and Carter Smith III. *Mapping Epidemics: A Historical Atlas of Disease.* New York: Franklin Watts, 2000.

Karlen, Arno. *Man and Microbes.* New York: G. P. Putnam's Sons, 1995.

Lerner, Robert E., et al. *Western Civilizations.* Vol 2. New York: W. W. Norton, 1988.

Porter, Roy, ed. *Cambridge Illustrated History of Medicine.* Cambridge: Cambridge University Press, 1996.

Rosenberg, Charles E. *The Cholera Years: The United States*

in 1832, 1849, and 1866. Chicago: The University of
     Chicago Press, 1987.

Snow, John. *On the Mode of Communication of Cholera.*
     London: John Churchill, New Burlington Street,
     England, 1855. (As reprinted at
     www.ph.ucla.edu/epi/snow/snowbook.html).

Wilkinson, Philip, and Michael Pollard. *Ideas That Changed
     the World: The Industrial Revolution.* New York: Chelsea
     House Publishers, 1995.

NOTES ON QUOTATIONS

The quotations in this book are from the following sources:

Chapter One: What Is Cholera?

p. 1: "I once marked down," Delaporte, *Disease and
     Civilization,* p. 43.

p. 4: "the lips blue," Durey, *The Return of the Plague,* p. 7.

Chapter Two: Life in the Time of Cholera

p. 9: "Where garbage," Lerner, *Western Civilizations,* p. 756.

p. 11: "It is by iron fingers," Editors of Time-Life Books,
     What Life Was Like in Europe's Romantic Era, p. 153.

p. 14: "It was," Durey, *The Return of the Plague,* p. 64.

Chapter Three: The Epidemic of 1831–1834

p. 22: "So, an epidemic arrives," Delaporte, *Disease and
     Civilization,* p. 11.

p. 22: "The accounts published," Durey, *The Return of the
     Plague,* p. 8.

p. 23: "state of collapse," Ibid., p. 28.

p. 24: "so black that its course," Ibid., p. 56.

p. 25: "ill-clad, ill-housed," Delaporte, *Disease and*

Civilization, p. 3.

p. 25: "narrow streets," Ibid., p. 11.

p. 27: *"Drunkards and filthy,"* Rosenberg, *The Cholera Years,* p. 44.

p. 29: "Avoid crude vegetables," Ibid., p. 30.

p. 29: "Numbers of our most accomplished ladies," Ibid., p. 31.

p. 31: "The common people," Durey, *The Return of the Plague,* p. 168.

p. 31: "I have never experienced," Ibid., p. 97.

p. 31: "The kindly affection of the father," Ibid., pp. 161–162.

p. 33: "Up the close and down the stair," www.crimelibrary.com/serial9/burke-hare

p. 34: "The roads, in all directions," Rosenberg, *The Cholera Years,* p. 28.

p. 34: "The cases of housebreaking," Ibid., p. 32.

p. 35: "The mercantile and shipping interests," Durey, *The Return of the Plague,* p. 143.

p. 35: "Cases of cholera," Ibid., p. 144.

Chapter Four: Cholera Strikes Again

p. 39: "Another spring will bring cholera," Rosenberg, *The Cholera Years,* p. 105.

p. 39: "no sooner had the impressive period," Durey, *The Return of the Plague,* p. 205.

p. 44: "the morbid material," Snow, *On the Mode of Communication of Cholera,* (as reprinted at www.ph.ucla.edu/epi/snow/snowbook.html), p. 13.

Chapter Five: Beyond the Broad Street Pump

p. 49: "Boil it," from www.cdc.gov Web site/Web page on cholera.

p. 51: "the cholera diarrhoea," Rosenberg, *The Cholera Years,* p. 195.

p. 51: "rigidly enforced precautions," Ibid., p. 195.

INDEX

**Page numbers for illustrations
are in boldface.**

ABOUT THE AUTHOR

STEPHANIE TRUE PETERS grew up in Westborough, Massachusetts. After graduating with a degree in history from Bates College, she moved to Boston, where she worked as an editor of children's books. She made the jump from editor to writer soon after the birth of her son. Since then, she has authored a number of nonfiction books for young people, including the other titles in the *Epidemic!* series. Stephanie lives in Mansfield, Massachusetts, with her husband, Dan, and their two children, Jackson and Chloe. She enjoys going on adventures with her family, beachcombing on Cape Cod, and teaching kick-boxing classes at the local YMCA.